Roly-Poly Ravioli

and Other Italian Dishes

by Nick Fauchald   illustrated by Ronnie Rooney

Special thanks to our content adviser:
Joanne L. Slavin, Ph.D., R.D.
Professor of Food Science and Nutrition
University of Minnesota

PICTURE WINDOW BOOKS
Minneapolis, Minnesota

Editors: Shelly Lyons and Christianne Jones   Designer: Tracy Davies
Page Production: Melissa Kes

Art Director: Nathan Gassman   Editorial Director: Nick Healy

The illustrations in this book were created with watercolor and pen and ink.

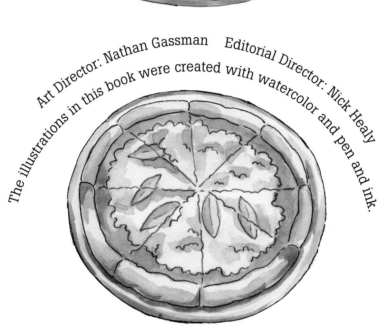

Picture Window Books • 151 Good Counsel Drive • P.O. Box 669 • Mankato, MN 56002-0669
877-845-8392 • www.picturewindowbooks.com

The illustration on page 4 is from *www.mypyramid.gov*.

Printed in the United States of America.

All books published by Picture Window Books are manufactured with paper containing at least 10 percent post-consumer waste.

Library of Congress Cataloging-in-Publication Data
Fauchald, Nick.
Roly-poly ravioli and other Italian dishes / by Nick Fauchald ; illustrated by Ronnie Rooney.
p. cm. — (Kids Dish)
Includes index.
ISBN 978-1-4048-5186-3 (library binding)
1. Cookery, Italian—Juvenile literature. I. Rooney, Ronnie, ill. II. Title.
TX723.F356 2009
641.5945—dc22   2008037908

Editor's note: The author based the difficulty levels of the recipes on the skills and time required, as well as the number of ingredients and tools needed. Adult help and supervision is required for all recipes.

Table of Contents

EASY

INTERMEDIATE

ADVANCED

MyPyramid

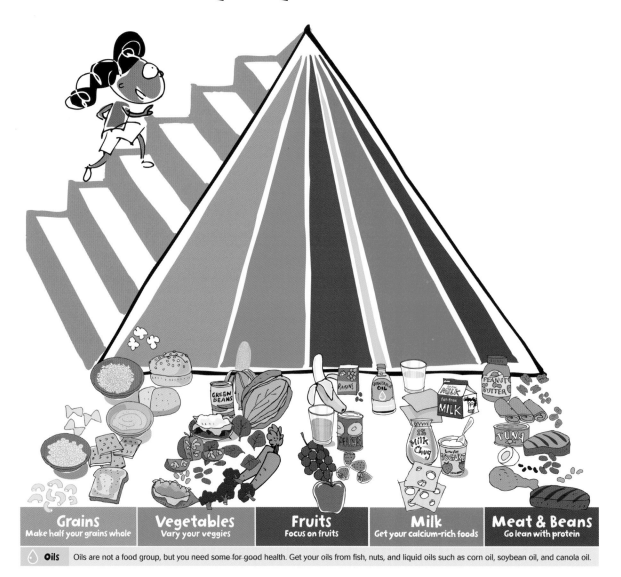

Grains	Vegetables	Fruits	Milk	Meat & Beans
Make half your grains whole	Vary your veggies	Focus on fruits	Get your calcium-rich foods	Go lean with protein

💧 **Oils** Oils are not a food group, but you need some for good health. Get your oils from fish, nuts, and liquid oils such as corn oil, soybean oil, and canola oil.

In 2005, the U.S. government created MyPyramid, a plan for healthy eating and living. The new MyPyramid plan contains 12 separate diet plans based on your age, gender, and activity level. For more information about MyPyramid, visit *www.mypyramid.gov*.

The pyramid at the top of each recipe shows the main food groups included. Use the index to find recipes that include food from the food group of your choice, major ingredients used, recipe levels, and appliances/equipment needed.

New York–based **Nick Fauchald** is the author of numerous children's books. He helped create the magazine *Every Day with Rachael Ray* and has been an editor at *Food & Wine* and *Wine Spectator* magazines. Nick attended the French Culinary Institute in Manhattan and has worked with some of the world's best chefs. However, he still thinks kids are the most fun to cook with.

Dear kids,

Do you like pizza? Spaghetti and meatballs? Many of America's favorite foods have their roots in Italy, a country that is famous for its food history. This cookbook will show you how to cook many of Italy's best dishes at home, with only a little help from an adult. Enjoy your meal, or as they say in Italy, "Buon appetito!"

Cooking is fun, and safety in the kitchen is very important. As you begin your cooking adventure, please remember these tips:

★ Make sure an adult is in the kitchen with you.
★ Tie back your hair and tuck in all loose clothing.
★ Read the recipe from start to finish before you begin.
★ Wash your hands before you start and whenever they get messy.
★ Wash all fresh fruits and vegetables.
★ Take your time cutting the ingredients.
★ Use oven mitts whenever you are working with hot foods or equipment.
★ Stay in the kitchen the entire time you are cooking.
★ Clean up when you are finished.

Now, choose a recipe that sounds tasty, check with an adult, and get cooking. Your friends and family are hungry!

Enjoy,
Nick

KIDS DISH

Note to Adults:

Learning to cook is an exciting, challenging adventure for young people. It helps kids build confidence; learn responsibility; become familiar with food and nutrition; practice math, science, and motor skills; and follow directions. Here are some ways you can help kids get the most out of their cooking experiences:

• Encourage them to read the entire recipe before they begin cooking. Make sure they have everything they need and understand all of the steps.

• Make sure young cooks have a kid-friendly workspace. If your kitchen counter is too high for them, offer them a step stool or a table to work at.

• Expect new cooks to make a little mess, and encourage them to clean it up when they are finished.

• Help multiple cooks divide the tasks before they begin.

• Enjoy what the kids just cooked together.

Special Tips and Glossary

cracking eggs: Tap the egg on the counter until it cracks. Hold the egg over a small bowl. Gently pull the two halves of the shell apart until the egg falls into the bowl.

measuring dry ingredients: Measure dry ingredients (such as flour and sugar) by spooning the ingredient into a measuring cup until it's full. Then level off the top of the cup with the back of a butter knife.

measuring wet ingredients: Place a clear measuring cup on a flat surface, then pour the liquid into the cup until it reaches the correct measuring line. Be sure to check the liquid at eye level.

blend: mix together completely

cool: set hot food on a wire rack or countertop until it's no longer hot

drain: pour off a liquid, leaving food behind; usually done with a colander

drizzle: lightly pour something over the top

layer: stack things one at a time

line: cover the inside of

mash: smash, usually with a fork, until the food is soft and separated

preheat: turn an oven on before you use it; it usually takes about 15 minutes to preheat an oven

roll: flatten with a rolling pin

shave: cut something into thin strips

slice: cut something into thin pieces

sprinkle: scatter something in small bits

stir: mix ingredients with a spoon until blended

toss: mix ingredients together with your hands or two spoons until blended

whisk: stir a mixture rapidly until it's smooth

METRIC CONVERSION CHART

1/4 teaspoon (1 milliliter)
1/2 teaspoon (2.5 milliliters)
1 teaspoon (5 milliliters)
2 teaspoons (10 milliliters)

1/4 tablespoon (4 milliliters)
1 tablespoon (15 milliliters)
2 tablespoons (30 milliliters)
3 tablespoons (45 milliliters)

1/4 cup (60 milliliters)
1/3 cup (80 milliliters)

1/2 cup (120 milliliters)
2/3 cup (160 milliliters)
3/4 cup (180 milliliters)
1 cup (240 milliliters)
1 1/2 cups (360 milliliters)
2 cups (480 milliliters)
3 cups (720 milliliters)

6 ounces (168 grams)
8 ounces (224 grams)
10 ounces (280 grams)
12 ounces (336 grams)

15 ounces (420 grams)

1/2 pound (225 grams)
1 pound (450 grams)

TEMPERATURE CONVERSION CHART

350° Fahrenheit (177° Celsius)
375° Fahrenheit (191° Celsius)
500° Fahrenheit (260° Celsius)

Kitchen Tools

8-by-8-inch metal baking pan

9-by-13-inch baking dish

aluminum foil

rimmed baking sheet

blender

butter knife

citrus juicer

colander

cooking spray

cooling rack

cutting board

clear measuring cup

fork

ice-cream scoop

kitchen shears

large pot

serving bowls

measuring cups

measuring spoons

microwave-safe bowl

mixing bowls

oven mitts

paper towels

pastry brush

pizza cutter

pizza pans

platter

rolling pin

rubber spatula

salad spoons

serrated knife

slotted spoon

small, sharp knife

spoons

toothpicks

vegetable peeler

whisk

wooden spoon

7

FRUITS, MILK

Semifreddo refers to any soft, almost-frozen dessert.

Berry Delicious Semifreddo

INGREDIENTS
1 1/2 cups frozen
    strawberries
1 cup mascarpone cheese
2 tablespoons
    confectioners' sugar
2 teaspoons vanilla extract

TOOLS
8-by-8-inch metal
    baking pan
blender
measuring cups
measuring spoons
rubber spatula
ice-cream scoop
serving bowls

1

Place an 8-by-8-inch metal baking pan in the freezer to chill.

2

Using a blender, blend the strawberries for 10 seconds, until finely chopped.

3

Add the mascarpone cheese, confectioners' sugar, and vanilla extract. Blend for 30 seconds.

4

With a rubber spatula, scrape the mixture into the baking pan.

FUN WITH FOOD★ Make the semifreddo with blueberries or raspberries, or mix all of the berries together!

5

Return the mixture to the freezer. Chill for 20 minutes, or until it's the texture of soft ice cream.

6 Scoop the semifreddo into small serving bowls and serve.

VEGETABLES, MILK

Insalata mista is Italian for "mixed salad."

Insalata Mista

INGREDIENTS
1 garlic clove
1/2 teaspoon salt, plus more
　for sprinkling
2 tablespoons
　balsamic vinegar
1/4 teaspoon freshly
　ground pepper
1/4 cup extra-virgin olive oil
one 8-ounce bag mixed
　Italian lettuce
1 medium carrot, peeled
1 wedge Parmesan cheese

TOOLS
medium mixing bowl
measuring spoons
fork
whisk
clear measuring cup
large mixing bowl
vegetable peeler
salad spoons

In a medium mixing bowl, sprinkle the garlic with salt, and mash it with a fork until it forms a paste.

Whisk in the vinegar, pepper, and 1/2 teaspoon salt.

Slowly drizzle the olive oil into the vinegar, whisking constantly.

Place the lettuce in a large bowl. With a vegetable peeler, shave the carrot into long ribbons. Add them to the lettuce.

FUN WITH FOOD★ To make this salad extra-healthy, add vegetables such as cucumbers, peppers, and tomatoes.

Drizzle the vinegar dressing over the lettuce. Toss the mix with salad spoons.

With a vegetable peeler, shave the Parmesan into thin ribbons.

Serve.

MILK, VEGETABLES

Caprese salad comes from the Isle of Capri in southwestern Italy.

Cool Caprese Salad

INGREDIENTS
3 tomatoes
1 pound fresh
   mozzarella cheese
coarse salt
1 bunch fresh basil
extra-virgin olive oil
freshly ground
   pepper (optional)

TOOLS
serrated knife
cutting board
platter

With a serrated knife, cut the tomatoes and mozzarella into slices. The slices should be about 1/4- to 1/2-inch thick.

Arrange the tomato slices on a platter. Lightly sprinkle the tomatoes with salt.

Top each tomato slice with a basil leaf or two.

Top each basil leaf with a slice of mozzarella.

NUTRITION NOTE★ Tomatoes are loaded with vitamin C. Vitamin C strengthens your immune system and helps your body absorb iron and calcium.

5

Drizzle olive oil over the mozzarella slices.

6 Sprinkle the salad with salt and pepper, and serve.

basil

GRAINS, MILK, MEAT & BEANS

Pesto is traditionally made by crushing herbs, garlic, and nuts in a bowl.

Pesto Perfecto

INGREDIENTS

2/3 cup extra-virgin
   olive oil
3 large garlic cloves
1/2 cup pine nuts
3 cups loosely packed
   fresh basil
2/3 cup freshly grated
   Parmesan cheese
1 tablespoon fresh
   lemon juice
1 teaspoon salt
1/2 teaspoon freshly
   ground black pepper
1 pound penne pasta

TOOLS

blender
clear measuring cup
measuring cups
measuring spoons
rubber spatula
large pot
colander
large serving bowl
wooden spoon

1 In a blender, blend the olive oil, garlic, pine nuts, and basil until they all are finely chopped.

2 Scrape the inside of the blender with a rubber spatula. Add the Parmesan, lemon juice, salt, and pepper. Blend the mix until smooth.

3 Ask an adult to cook the pasta in boiling salted water until the noodles are *al dente*, or firm.

4 Have an adult drain the pasta and pour it into a large bowl.

5 Add the pesto, and stir it into the pasta.

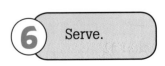

6 Serve.

Bruschetta can be any combination of grilled or toasted bread and a variety of toppings.

Tasty Tuna Bruschetta

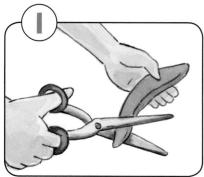

1

With a kitchen shears, cut the red peppers into small pieces.

2

Tear the parsley leaves into small pieces.

3

In a medium bowl, use a fork to mix the tuna with the peppers, parsley, capers, olive oil, and lemon juice. Season to taste with salt and pepper. Refrigerate until ready to use.

4

Ask an adult to toast the bread. Rub each piece of toasted bread with a piece of garlic. Lightly drizzle the bread with olive oil.

5

Spoon the tuna topping onto the toasted bread.

6 Serve.

INGREDIENTS

2 roasted red peppers from a jar, drained
20 flat-leaf parsley leaves
one 6-ounce can oil-packed tuna, drained
1 tablespoon capers, drained
3 tablespoons extra-virgin olive oil, plus more for drizzling
2 tablespoons fresh lemon juice
salt and freshly ground black pepper
8 slices Italian bread
1 garlic clove, cut in half

TOOLS

kitchen shears
medium mixing bowl
fork
measuring spoons
spoon
platter

15

Panini is Italian for "little breads."

Pile-It-On Panini

INGREDIENTS

one 8-ounce ball fresh
   mozzarella cheese
1/4 cup store-bought
   olive tapenade
four 6-inch-long pieces of
   ciabatta or Italian bread,
   cut in half
4 slices prosciutto
12 large basil leaves

TOOLS

serrated knife
cutting board
measuring spoons
rimmed baking sheet
oven mitts
platter

Preheat oven to 350°.

Using a serrated knife, cut the mozzarella into 8 slices.

Spread 1 tablespoon of olive tapenade on half of a piece of bread.

Lay a slice of prosciutto on top of the tapenade. Top the prosciutto with two slices of mozzarella.

5

Top the mozzarella with three basil leaves. Place a second half of bread on top and press down. Place the sandwich on a rimmed baking sheet.

6

Repeat steps 3–5 with the remaining ingredients to make four sandwiches.

7

Ask an adult to bake the panini until the cheese begins to melt, about 8 minutes.

8 Let the panini cool slightly, then serve it on a platter.

This Recipe Includes

FRUITS

Granita is an icy dessert that originated in Sicily, an island in southern Italy.

Chilly Lemon Granita

INGREDIENTS

7 lemons
2 cups water
3/4 cup sugar

TOOLS

8-by-8-inch metal
    baking pan
cutting board
serrated knife
citrus juicer
clear measuring cup
measuring cups
blender
fork
ice-cream scoop
serving bowls

1

Place an 8-by-8-inch metal baking pan in the freezer to chill.

2

Cut the lemons in half and juice them (you should have about 1 cup of juice).

3

Place the lemon juice, water, and sugar in a blender. Blend the ingredients for about 1 minute, until the sugar is dissolved.

4

Pour the mixture into the baking pan and freeze for 30 minutes.

FUN WITH FOOD★ You can make this granita with your favorite fruit juice, such as orange or grape.

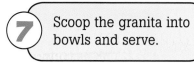

7 Scoop the granita into bowls and serve.

Remove the pan from the freezer. Stir the mixture with a fork, breaking up any large clumps. Return the pan to the freezer.

Repeat step 5 every 30 minutes, until the mixture is slushy throughout, about 2 hours.

GRAINS, MILK,
MEAT & BEANS

Strata is a traditional Italian breakfast casserole.

Sun-Is-Up Strata

INGREDIENTS

6 thick slices Italian bread
1/2 pound uncooked pork
    sausage meat, crumbled
one 8-ounce bag shredded
    cheddar cheese
6 large eggs
2 cups milk
1 teaspoon ground
    dry mustard
1 teaspoon salt
1/2 teaspoon freshly
    ground black pepper

TOOLS

cooking spray
8-by-8-inch metal
    baking pan
large mixing bowl
measuring cups
clear measuring cup
measuring spoons
whisk
oven mitts
toothpick
small, sharp knife
serving plates

Preheat the oven to 375°.

Grease the 8-by-8-inch baking pan
with cooking spray. Tear the bread
into large cubes. Cover the bottom
of the pan with half of the bread.

Sprinkle half of the sausage and
cheese over the bread.

Add the rest of the bread cubes.
Sprinkle the remaining sausage
and cheese on top.

20

5 In a large bowl, whisk the eggs with the milk, dry mustard, salt, and pepper.

6 Pour the egg mixture over the bread mixture.

7 Gently press on the bread, so it soaks up the egg mixture.

8 Ask an adult to bake the strata for about 1 hour, or until a toothpick inserted into the center comes out clean.

9 Cool the strata for 10 minutes. Cut it into squares and serve.

Ravioli is traditionally made with thin squares of fresh pasta.

Roly-Poly Ravioli

INGREDIENTS

1 cup ricotta cheese

1 egg

1/4 tablespoon flat-leaf parsley leaves

1/2 teaspoon salt

1/4 teaspoon freshly ground pepper

1/2 cup freshly grated Parmesan cheese

one 12-ounce package wonton wrappers or gyoza skins

1 cup warm pasta sauce

TOOLS

blender

measuring cups

measuring spoons

small bowl

pastry brush

large pot

slotted spoon

paper towels

platter

1 In a blender, blend the ricotta with the egg, parsley, salt, pepper, and Parmesan cheese until combined, about 10 seconds. Place the mixture in the refrigerator. Chill it for 20 minutes.

2 Place 24 wonton wrappers on a work surface. Fill a small bowl with water. With a pastry brush, lightly brush the wrappers with water.

3 Place 1 tablespoon of the ricotta filling on each of the wonton wrappers. Top with another wonton wrapper.

4 Using your fingers, push out any air bubbles. Press the edges of the wrappers together to make a tight seal.

5

Ask an adult to cook the ravioli, a few at a time, in simmering salted water for 2 minutes. The ravioli will rise to the surface and be tender.

6

With a slotted spoon, transfer the ravioli to paper towels to drain.

7 Place the ravioli on a platter. Pour pasta sauce over the ravioli and serve.

This Recipe Includes
GRAINS, MILK, VEGETABLES

Lasagna comes from the Italian word for the dish in which it's cooked.

Cheesy Spinach Lasagna

INGREDIENTS
3 cups pasta sauce
9 no-boil lasagna noodles
one 15-ounce container
    non-fat ricotta cheese
one 8-ounce bag shredded
    mozzarella cheese
one 10-ounce package
    frozen chopped spinach,
    thawed and squeezed dry

TOOLS
9-by-13-inch baking dish
clear measuring cup
rubber spatula
spoon
oven mitts

1 Preheat the oven to 375°.

2 Spread one-third of the pasta sauce over the bottom of the 9-by-13-inch baking dish with a spatula. Top with an even layer of three lasagna noodles.

3 Spoon one-third of the ricotta over the noodles.

4 Sprinkle one-third of the mozzarella over the ricotta.

24

NUTRITION NOTE★ Spinach is full of vitamins and iron that help keep your energy high.

5

Place one-third of the spinach over the cheeses.

6

Repeat steps 2–5 to make two more layers. Spread the pasta sauce over the cheese and spinach on each layer.

7

Ask an adult to bake the lasagna for 40 minutes.

8 Let the lasagna cool for 15 minutes before serving.

This Recipe Includes

VEGETABLES, GRAINS, MEAT & BEANS, MILK

Spaghetti means "little strings" in Italian.

Spaghetti and Meatballs

INGREDIENTS

1/2 pound ground beef
1/2 pound ground pork
1 large egg
1/3 cup bread crumbs
1/4 cup grated Parmesan
   cheese, plus more
   for serving
1 teaspoon garlic powder
2 teaspoons Dijon mustard
2 cups pasta sauce
1 teaspoon salt
1 pound spaghetti

TOOLS

rimmed baking sheet
aluminum foil
cooling rack
large mixing bowl
measuring cups
measuring spoons
microwave-safe bowl
large pot
oven mitts
colander
large serving bowl
two spoons

Preheat the oven to 375°. Line a rimmed baking sheet with aluminum foil, and place a cooling rack on top of it.

In a large mixing bowl, use your hands to mix the beef with the pork, egg, bread crumbs, Parmesan, garlic powder, and mustard.

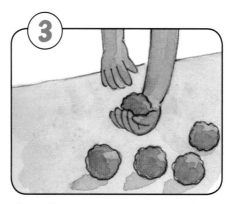

Form the meat mixture into about 20 balls, each about 1 inch across.

Place the meatballs on the rack. Ask an adult to bake the meatballs until browned and cooked through, about 30 minutes.

FOOD FACT *Al dente* is Italian for "to the tooth." It's a term for explaining how Italians like their pasta cooked: firm and not too mushy (and definitely not crunchy).

5 Meanwhile, pour the pasta sauce into a microwave-safe bowl. Ask an adult to heat the pasta sauce in the microwave until warmed through, about 60 seconds.

6 Ask an adult to cook the spaghetti in boiling salted water until al dente.

7 Have an adult drain the pasta and place it in a serving bowl.

8 Add the sauce and meatballs to the pasta. Toss until sauce coats the noodles.

9 Serve the spaghetti with extra Parmesan on the side.

This Recipe Includes

VEGETABLES, GRAINS, MEAT & BEANS, MILK

Stromboli is named after a tiny island off the coast of Sicily, in southern Italy.

stromboli

INGREDIENTS

3 roasted red peppers
   from a jar, drained
all-purpose flour,
   for dusting
1-pound piece of
   pizza dough
6 slices ham
6 slices provolone cheese
6 slices salami
8 large basil leaves
1 large egg, lightly beaten

TOOLS

cooking spray
rimmed baking sheet
kitchen shears
rolling pin
small bowl
pastry brush
oven mitts
cooling rack
serrated knife
platter

1
Preheat the oven to 375°.
Grease the baking sheet with
cooking spray.

2
Using a kitchen shears, cut the red
peppers into 1/2-inch-wide strips.

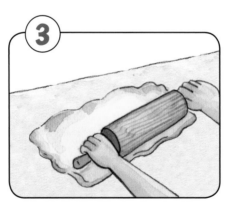

3
On a lightly floured surface, roll
out the pizza dough into a
10-by-13-inch rectangle.

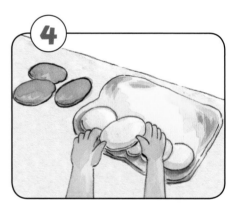

4
With a long side of the dough
facing you, layer the ham,
provolone, and salami across the
bottom half, leaving a 1/2-inch
border across the bottom.

28

FOOD FACT★ A stromboli is sometimes called a
calzone. It is a pocket of dough filled with a variety
of meats, cheeses, and vegetables.

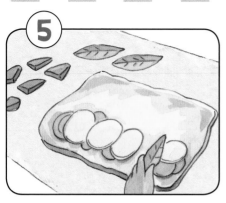

5 Layer the basil leaves and roasted red peppers over the meat and cheese.

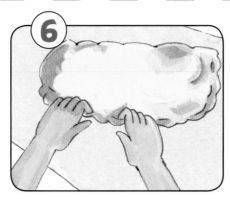

6 Loosely roll the dough, and tuck the ends under. Pinch the seams together to seal.

7 Place the stromboli on the baking sheet, seam side down. Brush it lightly with the beaten egg.

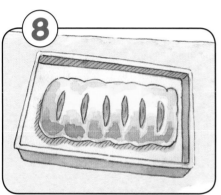

8 With a kitchen shears, make 6 slits across the top of the dough.

9 Ask an adult to bake the stromboli for about 40 minutes, until golden brown.

10 Transfer the stromboli to a cooling rack. Let it cool for 20 minutes before slicing and serving.

ADVANCED
Number of Servings: two 12-inch pizzas
Ready to Eat: 30 minutes

VEGETABLES, GRAINS, MILK

Pizza Margherita is named after a 19th-century queen of Italy, Queen Margherita.

Pizza Margherita

INGREDIENTS

all-purpose flour
1 pound pizza dough
1 cup tomato sauce
12 large basil leaves
1/2 cup freshly grated
    Parmesan cheese
1/2 pound fresh mozzarella
    cheese, thinly sliced

TOOLS

two large pizza pans
rolling pin
measuring cups
rubber spatula
oven mitts
pizza cutter

1 Preheat oven to 500°. Lightly sprinkle two large pizza pans with flour.

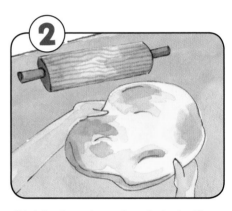

2 Divide the pizza dough in half. Roll and stretch the dough into two 12-inch circles. Place each circle on a pizza pan.

3 Using a spatula, spread 1/2 cup of sauce evenly on each pizza. Leave a 1/2-inch border around the edges of the dough.

4 Place six basil leaves on top of each pizza.

FUN WITH FOOD★ Change it up! Pizza Margherita has only three toppings. You can add your favorite toppings and rename the pizza after yourself!

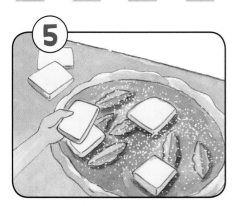

5

Sprinkle 1/4 cup of the Parmesan cheese over each pizza and top with the mozzarella slices.

6

Ask an adult to bake the pizzas for about 9 minutes, or until the cheese is bubbling and the edges are golden brown.

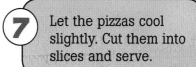

7 Let the pizzas cool slightly. Cut them into slices and serve.

INDEX

ON THE WEB

FactHound offers a safe, fun way to find educator-approved Internet sites related to this book.

Here's what you do:
  1. Visit *www.facthound.com*
  2. Choose your grade level.
  3. Begin your search.

This book's ID number is 9781404851863.

DATE DUE

DEMCO, INC. 38-3011